Highlights

Christmas Hidden Pictures Puzzles to Highlight

HIGHLIGHTS PRESS
Honesdale, Pennsylvania

needle

tube of toothpaste

peanut

egg

banana

teacup

candy cane

carrot

comb

ghost

2

muffin   doughnut   flipper   lightbulb   ice-cream cone   bell

matchstick   crown   high-heeled shoe   flashlight   closed umbrella

lightning bolt

musical note

muffin

lock

lollipop

drumstick

candy corn

canoe

rake

boomerang

leaf

heart

wedge of cheese

wedge of lemon

flipper

hot dog

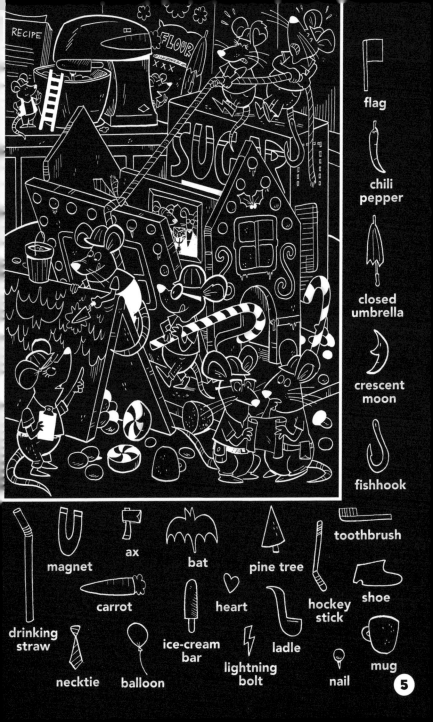

RECIPE
FLOUR
SUGAR

flag

chili pepper

closed umbrella

crescent moon

fishhook

magnet

ax

bat

pine tree

toothbrush

drinking straw

carrot

heart

hockey stick

shoe

necktie

balloon

ice-cream bar

lightning bolt

ladle

nail

mug

5

baseball bat

stick of gum

pencil

staple

heart

nail

measuring cup

flag

sailboat

pea pod

bowl

lollipop

water bottle

candle

sock

slice of pie

leaf

crescent moon

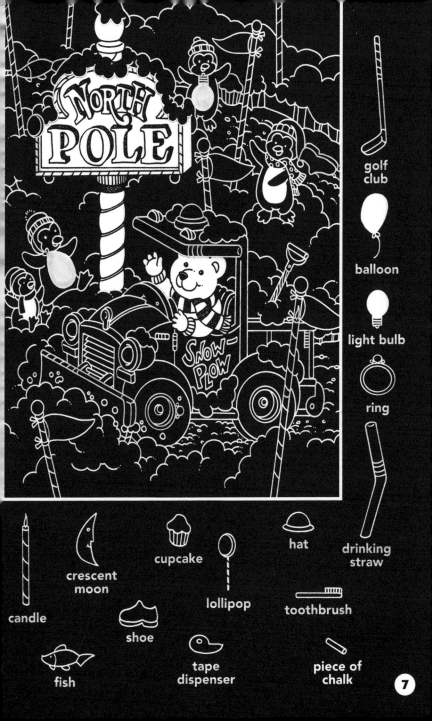

NORTH POLE

SNOW PLOW

golf club

balloon

light bulb

ring

drinking straw

hat

cupcake

crescent moon

lollipop

toothbrush

candle

shoe

tape dispenser

piece of chalk

fish

envelope

chef's hat

seashell

coat hanger

ghost

candy kiss

game piece

slice of bread

dolphin

8

flashlight heart broccoli book peanut

turtle spool of thread yo-yo fish horseshoe chili pepper candy cane

9

hot dog

mug

party
hat

candy
cane

muffin

seashell

crown

ice-cream
cone

carrot

horseshoe

doughnut

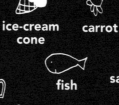
fish

saltshaker

slice of
pie

pear

slice of
bread

fork

hamburger

mushroom

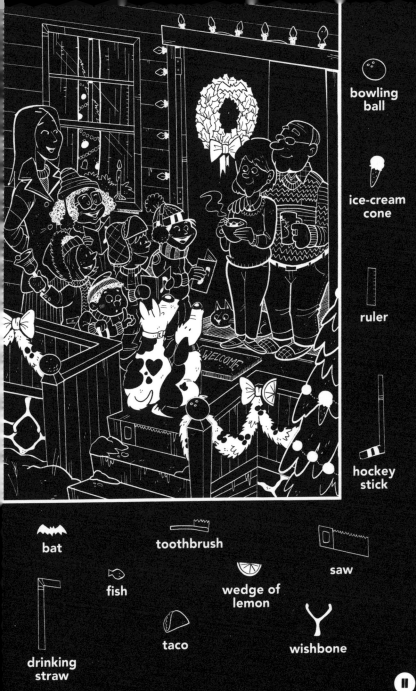

bowling ball

ice-cream cone

ruler

hockey stick

bat

toothbrush

saw

fish

wedge of lemon

taco

wishbone

drinking straw

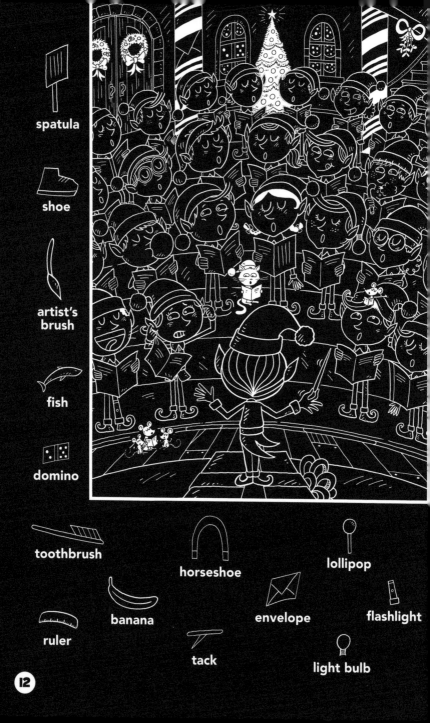

spatula

shoe

artist's brush

fish

domino

toothbrush

horseshoe

lollipop

ruler

banana

envelope

flashlight

tack

light bulb

seashell

pepper

crescent moon

candle

heart

nail

envelope

boomerang

slice of pizza

butter knife

book

arrow

funnel

canoe

shoe

wishbone

chili pepper

sailboat

13

shuttlecock

top hat

test tube

crescent moon

flag

drum

leaf

kite

spool of thread

ruler

crown

seashell

question mark

crayon

oar

tube of toothpaste

comb

15

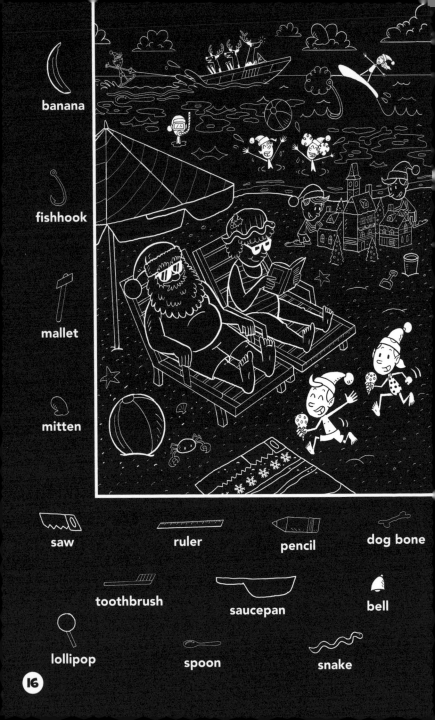

banana

fishhook

mallet

mitten

saw

ruler

pencil

dog bone

toothbrush

saucepan

bell

lollipop

spoon

snake

handbell

book

pencil

ring

ice-cream cone

bugle

saw

sock

sailboat

football

crown

scissors

17

dinosaur jellyfish comb sailboat mushroom elephant fork fish

spatula crown heart jump rope cactus

butterfly

envelope

candle

bell

magic wand

wishbone

gingerbread man

ice-cream bar

ladle

tent

star

shoe

19

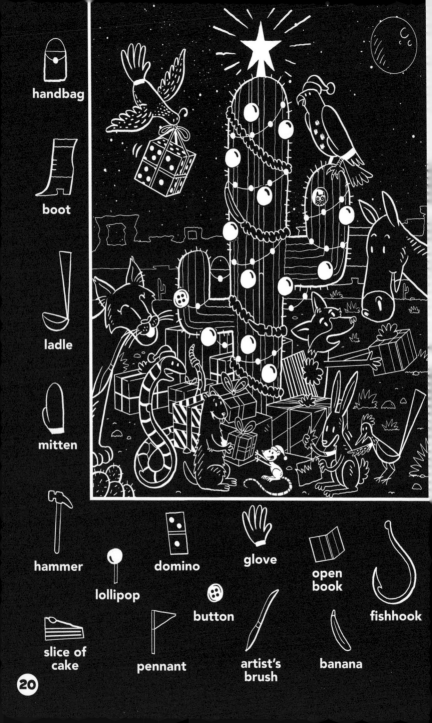

handbag

boot

ladle

mitten

hammer

lollipop

domino

button

glove

open book

fishhook

slice of cake

pennant

artist's brush

banana

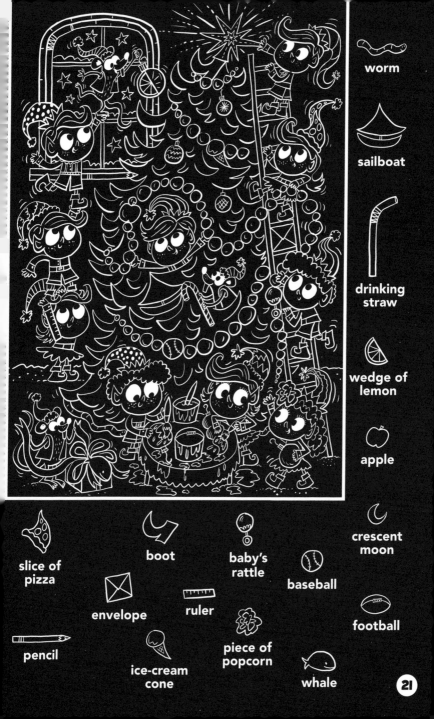

worm

sailboat

drinking straw

wedge of lemon

apple

crescent moon

slice of pizza

boot

baby's rattle

baseball

envelope

ruler

football

pencil

ice-cream cone

piece of popcorn

whale

Christmas Trees

ruler

button

top hat

envelope

baseball glove

pear

broccoli

ice-cream cone

toothbrush

fork

22

slice of pizza

wedge of lemon

eyeglasses

comb

football

chili pepper

crayon

crown

exclamation point

ice-cream cone

crescent moon

bowl

game piece

candle

ship

sock

top hat

bird

ladder

dinosaur

beet

ring

flag

ring

chili pepper

stick of gum

glove

teacup

dog dish

cinnamon bun

crescent moon

envelope

fishhook

crown

funnel

pennant

boomerang

slice of pie

pencil

arrow

paper clip skateboard slice of pizza pencil tube of toothpaste

envelope saucepan fishhook ruler handbag peanut

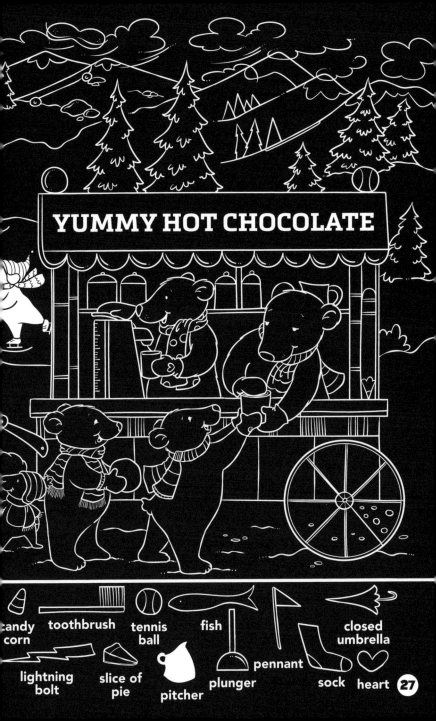

YUMMY HOT CHOCOLATE

candy corn · toothbrush · tennis ball · fish · closed umbrella · lightning bolt · slice of pie · pitcher · plunger · pennant · sock · heart

ruler

magic wand

mug

lollipop

slice of pie

ice-cream cone

hockey stick

golf club

envelope

sock

comb

telescope

doughnut

toothbrush

cupcake

saltshaker

Page 4

Page 5

Page 6

Page 7

Page 10

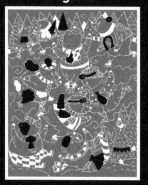

Page 11

Page 12

Page 13

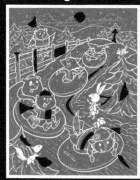

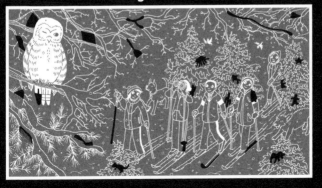

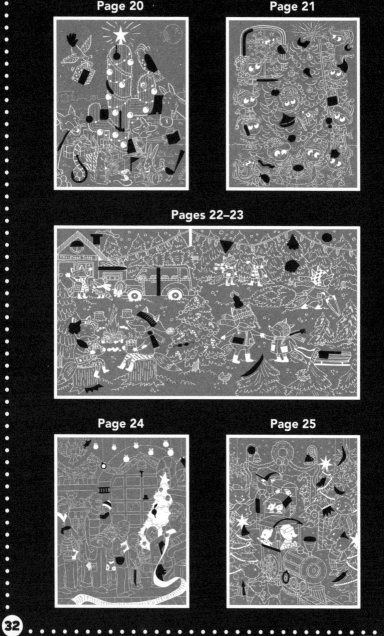